Dear Family,

What's the best way to help your child love reading?

Find good books like this one to share—and read together!

Here are some tips.

●**Take a "picture walk."** Look at all the pictures before you read. Talk about what you see.

●**Take turns.** Read to your child. Ham it up! Use different voices for different characters, and read with feeling! Then listen as your child reads to you, or explains the story in his or her own words.

●**Point out words as you read.** Help your child notice how letters and sounds go together. Point out unusual or difficult words that your child might not know. Talk about those words and what they mean.

●**Ask questions.** Stop to ask questions as you read. For example: "What do you think will happen next?" "How would you feel if that happened to you?"

●**Read every day.** Good stories are worth reading more than once! Read signs, labels, and even cereal boxes with your child. Visit the library to take out more books. And look for other JUST FOR YOU! BOOKS you and your child can share!

The Editors

For Bernette and George
—SB
To Rebecca Erin
—CVW and YHH

Text copyright © 2004 by Sonia W. Black.
Illustrations copyright © 2004 by Cornelius Van Wright and Ying-Hwa Hu.
Produced for Scholastic by COLOR-BRIDGE BOOKS, LLC, Brooklyn, NY
All rights reserved. Published by SCHOLASTIC INC.
JUST FOR YOU! is a trademark of Scholastic Inc.

ISBN 0-439-56878-1

Library of Congress Cataloging-in-Publication Data is available.

10 9 8 7 6 5 4 3   04 05 06 07 08

Printed in the U.S.A.   23

First Scholastic Printing, April 2004

Jumping the Broom

by Sonia W. Black

Illustrated by Cornelius Van Wright
and Ying-Hwa Hu

JUST FOR YOU!™
Level 3

There was lots of excitement at Erin's house. Her big sister Simone was getting married on Saturday.

Aunts and uncles and cousins who lived far away had come to town for the wedding, all bearing gifts. Everyone was so happy!

Everyone, that is, except Erin. She should have been happy, too.

Erin was going to be the flower girl. She loved her big sister, and she would miss her. But she *was* getting Simone's old room!

She loved her sister's fiancé, too—Jamal was cool!

Yesterday, Erin's grandmother had come to stay! What more could Erin want?

All by herself, Erin wandered into the living room. She looked again at the huge pile of wedding gifts. "I want to give Simone a gift, too," she said to herself. "I want to give her something special."

For the tenth time that week, Erin counted the money in her shoebox savings bank. It was still not enough to buy something really special for Simone.

Erin walked slowly into the kitchen.
Her grandmother was there with the others,
cooking, laughing, and chatting away.

"Why the sad face, Erin?" Nana asked.
"Come, tell me all about it."

In her room, Nana sat Erin on her lap, just as she used to do when Erin was small. "Now, what's the matter, little one?" Nana asked.

Erin snuggled close to Nana and let it all out. "I don't have enough money to buy a gift for Simone!" she cried.

"Simone won't mind that you can't buy her a gift, honey!"

"But I *want* to give her something, Nana," said Erin. "So she won't forget me!"

Nana gave Erin a big hug. "How could your sister forget *you?*"

Suddenly Erin noticed an old photo album lying open on the bed.

"I was looking at *my* wedding photos," Nana said.

"You looked so pretty, Nana!"

"I wore my mother's wedding dress," said Nana, adding softly, "and the necklace was your grandpa's wedding gift to me."

On the next page, there was a photo of Nana and Grandpa, arm in arm.

"Here we are 'jumping the broom!'" said Nana.

"Jumping the broom?" asked Erin.

"It's an old tradition we keep in our family," Nana said, pointing to an old straw broom that was standing in the corner.

Nana explained: "Long ago, when black people were brought here from Africa as slaves, it was against the law in some states for blacks to marry in church. So we made up our own ceremony. At the end, the couple jumped over a broom!"

"But why, Nana?" asked Erin.

"It meant they were jumping the broom into their new life together. Nowadays, more and more couples are jumping the broom to carry on that special tradition! Your mama did it with my broom, and Simone will use it in her wedding, too."

When Nana finished her story, Erin jumped up and clapped her hands. "I know the perfect wedding gift for Simone!" she cried. "Nana, will you help me?"

"Of course I will, if I can," Nana answered. So Erin told Nana her idea.

Early the next morning, Nana drove Erin
to the craft store. Erin carried her shoebox,
and a list she had made the night before.

She took a long time choosing each thing
she wanted to buy.

At last she was finished—and she had just
enough money for everything!

They hurried back home. Upstairs in
Nana's room, Erin spread out everything she
had bought on the floor. Then she got down
to work with scissors and glue and needles
and thread.

By afternoon, she let Nana in to see what she had made. "I'm all done!" said Erin.

"Good job!" said Nana. "Let's give Simone our gifts tomorrow."

"Yes," said Erin, "on her wedding day! But what's yours, Nana?"

Nana winked. "You'll have to wait and see."

Finally, tomorrow came! Nana called
Simone to her room.

Simone looked so pretty in her wedding
gown—like an African princess.

"Wow!" said Erin. "You look awesome!"

"So do you, little flower girl!" said Simone.

"Simone, dear," said Nana, "here is my gift. I hope you'll enjoy it as much as I have."

Erin's eyes grew big with surprise.

"Your pearl necklace from Grandpa!" Simone cried. "Thank you so much, Nana!"

"Erin, don't you have a gift for Simone?" asked Nana.

From behind her back, Erin brought out Nana's old broom. But now it was beautiful! "I decorated it myself," whispered Erin.

Cowry shells and little bells jingled as she gave the broom to her sister.

Simone's eyes filled with tears. "This is so special, Erin," she said. "Jamal and I will hang it up in our new home—and we'll keep it for you until *you* get married!"

Simone gave Nana and Erin a big hug.
"Now," she said, "let's get to the church
so I can jump the broom!"

▲▲▲▲▲ JUST FOR YOU ▲▲▲▲▲

Here are some fun things for you to do.

What's Cooking?

Before the wedding, Erin's family cooks up a storm! When people get together to celebrate, good food is often part of the fun.

Imagine that your family is having a party. What foods would be part of YOUR celebration?

Write a menu! List all the good food you would want to have at your party. Draw a picture of your family enjoying the feast YOU planned.

Made by YOU, With Love!

Erin made a very special gift for Simone by decorating the broom herself.

Think of a special gift YOU could make for someone you care about.

Draw a plan to show what the gift would look like. Then write a sentence telling who would get this special gift, and why.

Every Picture Tells a Story

Did you notice that the last two pages of this story have no words? The picture says it all. Or does it?

What do YOU think Erin is feeling as she watches her sister jump the broom? Pretend that you are Erin's friend and you are there, too. Write your own story about the wedding. What happens is up to YOU!

▲▲▲▲TOGETHER TIME ▲▲▲▲

Make some time to share ideas about the story with your young reader. Here are some activities you can try. There are no right or wrong answers!

Talk About It: Erin learns a lot when she looks at Nana's photo album. If you have old family photos you can share with your child, look at them together. Talk about what is happening in each picture. If you don't have any photos, tell your child a story about a happy day from your past. Then ask your child to talk about about a good time he or she remembers.

Think About It: Ask your child, "Why do you think jumping the broom is so important to Erin, Simone, and Nana?" Explain that a *tradition* is something people do that gets passed down from generation to generation. Are there any traditions, or special ways of doing things, your family shares? Try to think of a new tradition you and your child can start together.

Read More: Visit your local library to find more stories about family traditions, such as *The Wedding* by Angela Johnson, *Juneteenth Jamboree* by Carole Boston Weatherford, and *We Had a Picnic This Sunday Past* by Jacqueline Woodson.

Meet the Author

SONIA W. BLACK says, "Jumping the broom is a special African-American custom, and its origin is important to our heritage. I wrote this story because I feel it is vital that we pass on information so age-old traditions can live on. Also—I just *love* weddings!"

Sonia was born in Kingston, Jamaica. When she was eleven, her family moved to Brooklyn, New York. Her love of writing began there, at PS 9, where she enjoyed creative writing classes with Miss Gibbs, a favorite teacher who read wonderful poetry and short stories aloud. After graduating from Wilmington College in Ohio, Ms. Black went to work for a publishing company and became a children's book editor. Her books for beginning readers include *Hanging Out With Mom*, *Plenty of Penguins*, and *Home for the Holidays*. Her other JUST FOR YOU! Book is *Mommy's Bed*. She lives in New Jersey with her two daughters, Greyson and Evanne.

Meet the Artists

CORNELIUS VAN WRIGHT and YING-HWA HU say, "We loved working on this story. On first reading, it seems to be a story about the tradition of jumping the broom. But when you read closely, it's so much more! It not only relates the fascinating history of this wedding tradition, but it's also about family, relationships, and renewing a legacy. Having so much in the story to work with made our job lots of fun!"

Cornelius and Ying-Hwa are a husband-and-wife team. They have been illustrating children's books since 1989. Cornelius studied at the School of Visual Arts in New York City. Ying-Hwa studied at Shi Chen College in Taiwan and St. Cloud University in Minnesota. Coming from different backgrounds, they love exploring many different cultures through children's books. Another book they illustrated in the JUST FOR YOU! series is *Singing For Dr. King* by Angela Shelf Medearis. They live in New York City with their daughter and son.